Ruin Me
Before the Party Ends

poems by

Chloe Rodriguez

Finishing Line Press
Georgetown, Kentucky

Ruin Me
Before the Party Ends

ACKNOWLEDGMENTS

I want to thank the following places for giving these poems a home outside of my
brain.

The Windward Review- "My Mother Teaches Me to Pick Spanish Moss"
The Delta Review- "My Porch Eaves Sing at Night"
Midnight Mind Magazine- "Churchill's is Gone. There Are No More Punk Dive Bars
in Miami Anymore" & "Tamiami Trail"

Publisher: Leah Huete de Maines
Editor: Christen Kincaid
Cover Art: Chloe Rodriguez
Author Photo: Bella Scoma, Scoma Photography
Cover Design: Elizabeth Maines McCleavy

Order online: www.finishinglinepress.com
         also available on amazon.com

Author inquiries and mail orders:
Finishing Line Press
PO Box 1626
Georgetown, Kentucky 40324
USA

Contents

The Pink Pussy Cat… 1

Ode for the Girls… 3

Ode to the Chicken Quesadilla at Taco Bell… 4

Churchill's is Gone. There Are No More Punk Dive Bars in

    Miami Anymore… 5

Ode to Nighttime Radio Host Delilah… 7

When an Older Man Explains Sexism to Me… 8

Ode for the Bad Bar Hook-Up… 10

Pop-Punk Princess Says… 11

Definitions, a Pantoum… 12

No Invitation to God's Country… 14

On Bottling Childhood… 16

My Porch Eaves Sing at Night… 18

Tamiami Trail… 19

Ode for the Alligator… 20

Driving South … 21

Driving at Sunset through the Everglades… 23

Ode to Laika… 25

My Mother Teaches Me to Pick Spanish Moss… 26

Inside the Killing Jar… 27

The Crystal Ball… 29

The Pink Pussy Cat

sat under the overpass of North River Drive
and 36th Street, roofless, a pastel pink façade.
A vestige of 1980s Miami, of big hair and
cocaine clouds and ecstasy laced with glitter,
the neon silhouettes of its nude dancing ladies
flickering fast n' slow, going in n' out like the
late-night vacancy signs of the motels that
lingered down the street with names like
PRINCESS, El Paraiso, or Starlite Executive
that advertise their Fantasy Showers, mirrored
ceilings, vibrating heart-shaped beds and
multi-jet sensual tubs in fine fluorescent print.
I don't remember the first time I saw that
enormous, eponymous pink building, but I do
remember sitting in the backseat of my mother's
white Honda Accord with the crank roll down
windows, thinking it was the most beautiful sight
I'd ever seen. In the early 2000s, with her lustful
eyes painted on the front door, beckoning you
in and on the expressway facing side, a mural
of painted ladies in strange positions like calligraphy
strokes curved this way n' that, an invitation
to the outside world of what waited in the
dimly lit drug den of illicit pleasures, full of
Miami's most wanted, n' the minxes n' the
foxy ladies who, if I was lucky enough, could see
a hundred feet above about to take their smoke
breaks and I dreamt of what they smelled like
in their tight, tiny clothes and their names and
what they did all day in the fun-house of the
Pink Pussy Cat that offered an all-day buffet.
When I'd ask my mother if it was a playground,
she'd always touch the rosary hanging off the
rearview mirror and say it was a palace of pleasures
for old, sleazy bikers who had nothing better to
fill their time. But now, when I drive past, the
building no longer shimmers like it used to,
the pink peels from its sides, and I can peer
inside like I've always wanted, to see old poles
covered in vines, n' drywall dust, torn-up leather
on stages hit hard n' faded by the Miami sun

without its top to cover up its sticky secrets.
They've painted her black to mourn the big cat,
n' the cocaine cowboys n' the cops. Renamed her
KRAVE, gave her inflatable legs with fishnets
and red bottoms for the roof. And now, when
I drive past, I think there should be nothing here
I don't remember, but she's grown quiet and dark,
a brooding widow in search of the *Old Miami*, asking
 newcomers what they crave, and all I can do is
remember and say *Hasta Luego Gatita Rosada* as I
drive down the Dolphin Expressway, searching
for memories in a foreign landscape that I
somehow still know, pretending, for a moment
longer, that I can see the ghosts of Miami's nightlife
dancing, raising their glasses in the motes of light,
coming in through the cracks, pink n' pulsing.

Ode for the Girls

O girls, girls, girls, O female fans
and bleacher creatures, we've been
named ring rats, shack rats, and
mat rats, the buckle bunnies,
puck bunnies, lot lizards, and
track tramps, dirt skirts, hoop hoes,
garage groupies, and tag chasers, the
good ol' hardwood honeys, punt or putt
bunnies, the pitch bitch, the barracks and
badge bunnies, the cleat chasers, the
cop-hoppers, or a lineman's favorite—
the bucket bunny, a hard-hat hussy,
of course, we can't forget our pit lizards, or
jersey grazers, the scene queens, and the
run 'em to the ground lacross-stitutes,
the book babes, sheet freaks, and chuckle fuckers.
Girls. Let's talk—woman to woman. Do you ever
wonder if, in the olden days, with the good mead
and woefully hygienic medieval times, if we were
more than just witches and wenches and harlots,
more than strumpets, giglots and tarts?
Think with me, girls. Could we have been the
tent trailers or lance lickers,the shield shaggers or
knight nailers, sword swallowers, and hilt hangers?
Maybe we were squire desirers, forge foxes, joust rabbits,
or Lancelot's lizards? Girls, we could have been
chain mail chasers, maile maidens, even a
codpiece cuddler? Perhaps even a shield maiden with
little care for combat? O' brazen babes, O' hags, O' girls,
girls, girls, we haven't changed, and why should we?

Ode to the Chicken Quesadilla at Taco Bell

I'd pick you over the sexiest lover
any time of the year. There's just
something oh-so romantic about
your extra creamy jalapeño sauce,
and your cheesy innards that make
the manic-pixie-dream girl I want to
be, inside me quiver over fake chicken
delight. Your tortilla is a better reminder
of a missed white lukewarm lover freckled
by the excess sun left out in my Florida
youth's sweet n' salty summer sidewalks.
O' Quesadilla, you, me, and a sweaty
Baja-blast could give Longinus the run
of his lifetime, trying to define the sublime
had he lived another 1750 years to meet
you n' me, sweetie. You take me back to
memories only unlocked by sauce packets
that ask for my hand in marriage, my
mother's voice and the smell of her
perfume in late-drive-thru lines with that
glaze that covered her eyes. O' three cheese
heaven, deemed the no. 7 you whisper
to me to think outside the bun and, baby
I do when the world is quiet, and it's just
us and maybe, just maybe, the memories
of my mother leak outside your cheese-glued
tortilla and miss the paper baggie that
cuffed you down for the ride home to stain
my pants in patterns that could be
confused for extra sodium-heavy tears
are when sacrilegious thoughts begin of
the bean burrito and the *better* times
with her and red sauce. O' T-bell, you
bittersweet slut, I'm on a diet, and
my therapist says I should manage my
triggers with more than just food, but
you're undeniable and available all
hours of the night, especially when
we can be tucked in together and
you whisper in my ear to live màs.

Churchill's is Gone. There Are No More Punk Dive Bars in Miami Anymore.

> *"If museums are places where art goes to die, then Churchill's is the place where art goes to get sloppy drunk, make a loud, hostile scene, and end up akimbo under a table, staring into its dark, gum-ridden underside. Then die."* —Rob Goyanes

No more navigating through men who settled
in the shadows or weaving through dumpsters
to see the porcelain glisten of drunk-drugged
eyes. Little Haiti-Rock City dead, no rhythm
hissing from neon or clanks from rusted fenders
in the old lot. No hands balled for riot or echos of
shitty, ear-blinding bands. No more Steve, white
Jesus, sore thumb in the crowd of misfits, passing
the sacred communion glass of acid-dropped
lemonade. Sweaty sock smell married to the fried
batter of fish and chips' oily air, mingling with smoke
and spilled PBR, never to linger in my hair again, never
to remind me of the night's blur. No cellophane crackling
of my skin, post-high plotting my second chances or
the failed smoking saints of the patio helping me paint
my own amnesia. Beer cans and peanut shells beneath
Doc Martens, their crinkles to go silent forever. The
Toilets to be cleaned, spackled white and pristine to cover
spray-painted walls, stickered to holy hell and back,
littered with needles, and cooked-clean spoons, not an
empty, beached solace baggie in sight. Long talks about
the moon or the meaning of life over shared joints or
bummed cigs left to idle, aimless in the humid heat,
drifting over the heads of us pub-going philosophers,
into the starry gates of the dark night. Never again a
green light shot salute to Ol' Churchill, his oil-painted
likeness that mantled the porta-potty pub heaven
entrance replaced by that damned neighborhood
Chili's sign, stripped from his majesty over and over.
The club faked their death so many times for attention,
they predicted their own fucking demise. The cocoon for
punks growing up in the city washed down the storm
drains by the bookoo bucks of capitalism. The oasis for
punk culture left unembraced by Miami, now a mirage,
shriveled, picked up by luxury cars, then spit out as

gravel on the drive down to Tobacco Road. The mohawks and chokers, the black nail polish, the mosh pits of love, the hot leather, the spikes, studs, patches, but most of all the punks, the punks will always be behind the barred windows of the pub, drinking and two-stepping with 'ol Churchill, throwing bottles and elbows, wasting and waiting on another show, another score, another home to rock in.

Ode to Nighttime Radio Host Delilah

Your smooth, sweet voice would slip from
the small holed speakers of my mother's
dashboard like honey oozing into the black
backseat, a bubble gum barrier, a safe zone
for sharing secrets. Delilah, you were my
mother's closest friend at the end of it all,
the late-night talks about grief and girlhood
or anything in between with her faucet eyes,
you made the 90s and 2000s a soft, yacht
rock ride that could sway me to sleep any day
of the week. Delilah, you were the yellowing
orange of the streetlamps past 10 PM and the
twinkling skyscraper stars far behind, moving
fast to your slow voice, the narrator of my
girlhood behind the game of tag played with
the silvery hue of the moon on cloudy nights.
Through the dark exits, with the potholes that
never got evened out, you mothered my mother,
with diet coke and reckless romance advice, and
maybe even a little sprinkle of Jesus here or there.
We'd park by payphones for your call-in philosophy,
waited for your jingle, the purl of ♪*De-li-lah* ♪
to fill the car with your warm voice of a hug,
whispering to love somebody tonight, with calm,
come-down energy, the gentle hush through
sleepless nights. O' Queen of sappy love songs
and puzzling it out, through Delilah's dilemmas,
to put it as you have, *Thank you, I'm glad you're here.*
The distant lights of my childhood never dimming.

When an Older Man Explains Sexism to Me

I sigh and let him go on, my mouth still open
from the mid interruption, force my tongue
to sleep and lie still, a bad habit still not broken.

My eyes shift downward, my voice, small, strained
stuck in the far behind of my throat, but he doesn't
notice my good girl silence or my folded legs or

the uncomfortable shift in my body when he uses the
words *Feminism, Patriarchy, Misogyny* as if they mean
the same thing. Interlaced in his one-sided "good guy"

conversation. I let him. Maybe he will tire, maybe he will
realize he is an active participant in the thing he claims to
hate most, maybe he will materialize into a white van, and I

will regret all the conversations I have had in the last 24
hours, maybe he will turn and ask me for the experience
of a woman, maybe he will pause hard at the pursing of

his lips before he says the word *pussy*. But he doesn't, he
continues spilling wrongs yet I still feel the words that are
dripping from his drunken mouth are and always will be

better than mine, they sound more elegant, wrapped up in
his mother's prettiest Sunday church dress, where he learned
to respect women but I'll remember he called his little sister's

friends *whores* and I won't correct him though I should.
We can both shove the gag in my mouth, wash the words
down my throat. He pats my shoulder, pushes out:

I totally empathize, hope you know I'm one of the good ones,
and takes a long swig of his beer as if he's just offered me
flowers that aren't already rotten that I do not have a vase

for other than my body. He gets up to get another drink,
and whispers *you're welcome* with a wink, and I spit out
thank you like a good woman who will hold his empty space

and pretend I have not wilted, my temporary beauty has not yet flushed from age or silence. Maybe I should remind him of the interruption. Maybe he will be "a good man" and say *Thank you.*

Ode for the Bad Bar Hook-Up

In the haziness of cheap liquor and neon glow
      with a harsh rhythm pulsating through sultry
air, I hope you agree it's best that what we did

      was left there to fester under the tainted floor
boards of the porcelain pony, an unclaimed
      and unnamed shitty art piece whose makers

reeked of the bottom shelf, tainted with faint whiffs
      of caramelized onion dip and the best of intentions.
Had it been any better, or had we been any older,

      it may have been mistaken for a Banksy, and then
we'd be stuck in a billion-dollar partnership, baby,
      but I'm glad you had no idea how to sign your initials

on my hip, at the lack of either one's ownership and
      that I fumbled with the paintbrush, even though you
sorta-kinda-liked it enough to ask for a selfie, us

      against the matte-black behind of the stall right
after the error of sin where you sneaked in some
      well-strungwords on bad IPA. The night grew

younger and we grew older, you shuffled through
      shaggy hair to find monikers for me and my
newfound meaning to you till I marked my memory

      on your neck to shut you up with a small red novelty
of newness for you, false promises of pleasing. You
      turned, enchanted, and I took my chance at leaving.

I'm sorry to say, I hope you waited all night, you, new
      philosophizer of the pub, with your IPA, thinking
of some future now lost, based on our misguided quest,
      dear stranger, it was really for the best.

Pop-Punk Princess Says

so you're done raging against the machine,
huh? you're a boring 25-year-old sell-out.
Already gave your performance of a lifetime?
Ha, you cheap trick, bi—Did you get your
fishnets in a twist up that checkered skirt,
Princess? Am I what's left of the gum you
tried to scrape off the hexagon bottoms of
your vans? Yeah,Yeah, Yeahs, whatever
happened to mosh pit courtesy, huh? If they
fall, pick 'em up. They want in? Let 'em in,
and if they want out, let 'em out. Pop-Punk
Princess says: *Remember high school? In the trunk*
of the car, we had Lorde's anthology, a bottle of Skol,
your stash, mace, and some cigarettes. Those were the
days when you stuck it to the man! You were a better
punk, I mean, person; let me save you! You need angst.
Oh yes, the days of crackle nail polish, rolling
spliffs, fried pink hair, a pass of hot vodka, and
house shows where we thought the drummer
would fall for us, if only he'd swoop his hair
the right way mid-set to catch my overlined
black eyes. Four Lokos forever, right? *Please!*
You bring the bleach, I'll bring chlorine! We can dye
our hair colors that nobody's ever seen. Sure, but
let's drop the pop. Burst your bubble fantasy.
I can just be the punk rock queen. I don't have
to be the rebel that you've wanted me to be;
you can pack up the records and cassettes, hang
up the combat boots, take off the crown, let's go
out to the bar, fuck, this song's stuck on repeat.
Can you back off, bitch? Don't cramp my style.

Definitions, a Pantoum

My mother promised promises were unbreakable,
words are glass, and if broken, they'll cut at will.
I often fumbled with words as a child,
she always chose hers with tact.

She said words are glass, and if broken, they cut at will.
Words are more than ink on paper & intended meaning.
She always chose hers with tact.
I began to read the dictionary daily.

Her words became more than just ink on paper with their intended meaning.
I looked up the definition of Mother.
I read the dictionary daily
Mother, a verb: to bring up (a child) with care and affection.

I defined the word Mother,
the words beneath it blatantly begged for attention.
Mother, (v): look after, a child, protectively, at times excessively with affection.
Her words always precise.

The words, a child, beneath it, blatantly begged for attention.
I stumbled across the word dependency
Mother's words always precise.
A person can be *dependent* on a substance without being addicted to it.

I fumbled with the word dependency.
Dependency meant two different things to us.
A person can be *dependent*, still resemble a mother, without being *addicted*.
That's how she chose to define *dependency*.

Dependency meant two different things for her and me.
She refused to define addiction
I believe this is how she chose to define *dependency*.
All the while she never stuttered.

She refused to define mother and her addictions,
her words became false triggers
yet, all the while, she never stuttered.
I waited for her words to cut her.

Words became a trigger,
at times they meant one thing, and then context changed.
I waited for her words to cut her.
My mother promised promises were unbreakable.

No Invitation to God's Country

I. South of the Dead Lakes, my body basks,
thoughtlessly, the black, sunned innertube
that floats without aim on the Chipola river.
The cackling of a motor, vapors of fuel drown
my stillness deep beneath the riverbanks.

Grasping the shore, remnants of a toppled swamp
gum tree, its underside speckled with lichen, inches
above the waterline. A shallow bank holding petrified
wood steppingstones, an anchor for my innertube.
I stop, bottom rooted on the bank, toes pulled by
the current, siren-serenading my body to follow.

The sun-induced sepia slowly fades in blinks,
transformed to ochre yellows. The river restored
to its clear gold flecked opal- blue beauty glazing
ghost limbs of fallen trees and scattered rock.

II. A man in polarized sunglasses atop a jonboat
drifts closer, rounding the riverbend. His wave,
and a thick southern drawl greet me, eyes peering
over the rims, anchoring himself by the sprawled,
dead roots of the gum tree. His mustache unveils a
devious smile. Snaggle toothed n' sharp toned he asks
What brings you out to God's Country?
Our eyes catching, I waited to answer.

III. As a child I hid under honeysuckle avoiding the
noontime sun, the burnt grass, sucking sugar from
the petals, salty sweat stuck to my skin. I took trips
to the graveyard with the preacher's daughter, where
even the gravestones didn't remember their names.
We picked forget-me-nots and pecked behind the
statue of St. Jude, patron saint of lost causes.

That summer passed; summers continued to pass.
They grew hotter, rained harder, each year till we never
visited our ancestors again, never exchanged glances
in church. Our secrets, told over the hum of cicadas
became whispers and vanished. They drowned with
her, trapped under the mangroves and the altar boy.

My mother played old vinyl that wailed church hymns
stories of the devil, made funeral casseroles and wore
black garb adorned with pearls. Said she went to church
"Just in case" and shook her head, her cross clinking
on her chest, *Just in case—Just in case—Just in case*
wearing dresses that folded between her legs like hands
pressed together in prayer when she sat on the pew.

IV. The preacher declared this land holy, calling out to
the lord almighty on the back porch where we once
smoked cigarettes, passed around mason jars of
moonshine, like ill-flavored grace on my tongue.
The flowers already smelled of rot. I burned my
bible to the sound of crickets. God stayed quiet,
the cicadas screamed their shrill warnings.

Great lunar moths would beat themselves dead
against our windows at night looking for the
light behind the pane. This was God's country,
but I stopped inviting him long ago.

I paused. Felt my breath flower at the back of my
throat and swallowed the thorns of my raspy breath.
Smiling, the words fell, rippling into the water
The change of scenery was inviting, I guess.

On Bottling Childhood
For Holly

Barefoot in the bluegrass, the
           embers of the dancing flames
fly, flickering against the night

           sky, earth-bound stars fading
into the heavy smoke of the bonfire
           and the cover of conversation.

Our sat silhouettes blur in n' out
           like soft static on the backdrop
of pruning barns painted black,

           hiding the mold of our forefathers
race with luck, hard mash, and the
           blessed drops of gold bourbon. We

tell stories of over the christening
           chorus of crickets and a large
mouthed mason jar. Our old little

           bodies now ghosts that run through
these fields, catching lightning bugs
           and giggling behind overgrown poplar

trees, now, where mules and horses
           throw their bodies on wet earth,
laboring machines, who go gentle

           and quiet in the thick of the night.
Skinned knees on asphalt and hands
           that smelled of dust and slight sweetness

from pushing freshly rounded hay bales
           onto unlit backroads, we were back
to the safety of tender grass behind rickety

wood fences, to watch for
oncoming trucks and pray that no one
        calls our fathers, knowing

our moms were far off, swimming
        in some kind of bottle, trapped
in its amber, too deep to care.

My Porch Eaves Sing at Night

with the croaks of frogs hitting high-low notes in the
southern silence and the American Spirit smoke curling
up to the crescent moon, I pull another from my blue
pack. In the distance, the coyotes cry, mimicking my
coughs to a campfire starred sky as I rock to and fro—
and to and fro—thinking of my father's Jesus, white
and prestigious. Magnolias sweeten the air, breathing
in the thick and humid. My breaths, almost wild, gasps
between puffs. The air this time of year never feels easy
to breathe. Its hot air, viscous charged with the electricity
of late summer storms, of nights spent indoors thinking.
Hoots of owls, and singing legs of crickets, long after the
hour of gloaming, remind me it isn't Sunday for two more
hours, so I convince myself there is still time for sinning.

Tamiami Trail

On a highway that meanders through the heart
of swamp & cypress & reservation, there is a green

stillness that leaks into your bones, lapping away
the frenzy of the city built by cocaine money, where

the road becomes a silver river splitting two lifelines.
There are banked alligators blackened by mud, wild

birds perched in mossy pine flatwoods, peering
with painted glass eyes, sentinels of the wetlands,

messengers from beyond the hand-crafted signs
by unsteady hands where the varying paints

read *swamp adventure, & sideshows & gifts*.
Chickee huts with the whispers of fry bread

or patient women braiding or cooking Sweetgrass,
where the ribboned river of grey & gravel pays

homage to the endless marshland that tongues the wet
horizon, where my heart has learned a steady rhythm.

Ode for the Alligator

who basks in the marshy median of the turnpike. Your
        oasis between hot tarmacs, a wet semblance of home.
Waiting for the fulfillment of your desires; beyond the
        journeyed success of our six laned suburbia. Your
mud-washed, black hide bared in the low water, eyes
        hidden behind partitions, suppressing a new hell,
a swamp-less, sun-soaked, human-cradled dystopia.

        You remain patient, peaceful, maw held open, a landing
strip awaiting a savory opportunity. I can hear your calls,
        the bellowing rising from the deep ache that vibrates within
you. I feel your yearning for the healing mud of the swamp
        to sink beneath the green tide of the Orphan Bayou, to be
unseen, unheard, for just a moment. I know the lonesome
        longing for people-less silence.

I too, wish for the human misstep, the quick glide into
        unsuspecting murk where they believe they can swim.
The quick dip, the close brush with the unstill water, how
        they wait for the fractals of capillary waves to heal, glaze
over, become the smoothed glass of comfort. Your orb eyes,
        nowhere to be seen. But you stalk them just below, listening
to their relief, misnaming God as their savior instead of you.

        In childhood, my Cajun neighbor told me stories of
the Letiches, the children abandoned and unbaptized
        raised by gators, their lost souls wandering the bayou.
You rest on the median, a mimic of what once belonged
        to you, outside gift shops that sell your skin in wallets,
your head as a paperweight far from any swamp.

        I will peer into your jagged smile, and I will listen to your
stranded song, the one I hear in dreams, where I creep
        into your open mouth, settle behind your tongue, breasts
to your belly, your body a wet warmth of home. I whisper
        to you, I beg you to take us to the sweet depths, into the
bosom of unseen life, where we will wait for the plumbing
        to give, for the panic, for the sinkholes to fill and fill, till
the brackish waters swallows all we've known brick by
        brick, tarmacs, strip malls and all. Sweet swamp baptism.
Until then, you wait on the median, and I drive by,
        both of us waiting and wasting on tomorrow.

Driving South

my mother, newly "rehabilitated"
groans from the backseat, and I look
out to empty highways and overpasses
and Southern Nothing. I'd spent the
night clawing at my chest to make
room for God, but these roadside
homilies erected by churches stood
next to signs, where I questioned
the possibilities in which I could have
driven into a parallel universe, TURN
RIGHT FOR FRIED CATFISH! paired
with Mary's eyes ever so watchful from
behind the safety of cement and the
greenery reminded me that this is just
podunk Florida, and many miles and
old churches with hollowed-out husks
for priests and dilapidated mobile homes
lay between me and ANGEL TEARS 1
MILE, the next rest stop, or the one
after that, or the one after that until I
pull into a driveway too long for just
my car, and she mumbles through the
silence *Jim Morrison is Alive, He Reads*
Fortunes from a Flea Market in Missouri.
My hot breath pulses against the one-sided
humid glass, I explain, Morrison died
in '71 but I'm interrupted by *do the crosses*
on the side of the highway ever get lonely? Well,
no, they have memories they keep guarded
as company, Mom. THE SWAMP IS REAL
passes to my left and to my right, a large
double billboard reads the blood of Jesus
cleanseth us from all sin and below Jesus is
Big Jim's Boobie Bungalow on exit 6 and a
new slew of signs flash penance and sins
splashing against the shades of dark veridian
with the sun fading behind WE BARE ALL,
and I ask her if she is hungry, has she eaten?
Do not ask for directions, if you do not know, distance
is measured in churches, Chloe, didn't you know God is
in all things? In my book, this is a yes for the

Taco Bell on exit 5 next to a citrus farm with
live baby gators. I peek at her from the rearview
as I pull off, THE SWAMP IS WATCHING she
sits up and whispers to me I'm just a full-bellied kitten
sleeping under God's porch, and he picks me up every evening
when he's smoking a cigarette and I think that in another
life, in a parallel world, I too am a fat cat, waiting,
just waiting for him to pull another from the pack.

Driving at Sunset through the Everglades

I am sitting in the passenger seat of the car with mud-tracked
Chuck Taylors, window to my right, the pane a partition, preserving,

& I am patient when he asks me if we can pull off the road. My eyelids furl
& unfurl, as I look out to the ever-growing fields of Saw Grass soaked in

nothing but sun, & mud, sincerity, & solitude. His right-hand rests in mine &
his arm becomes a log, floating along the skimpy hem of my skirt, feathered

by his red hairs that glisten in the sun's dying rays, littered with freckles as
lichen. His eyes caught in the kiss from the harbinger of heat, he who tongues

the watchful horizon. The orange-yellow flecks burnt into his larimar irises flightless,
& vibrating Lubber Grasshoppers who harmonize with one another after the hour of

gloaming. Where I've learned to accept what exists in the shadow, what is looming,
what is lurking; love, tied to tendrils of wild growth of mangroves. The fields of grass

are always the receiver. A wet prairie painted with the brushstrokes of birds, saged
with the timeless rain of Spanish moss that lingers, hovering, with its fingertips,

hanging from the Bald Cypress trees, waiting too, for its turn to stroke the water that
rests. Slow-moving, rising waters, sweet summer birthplace of love, baptized in steady

sweat from humid heat. I watch the gesturing 'Glades teach me acceptance & perseverance,
how to remain strong & natural, uninviting & dangerous, how to beckon him to sink beneath

the murky waterline, to hold our breath for even just a minute. Or awareness, a prickled
feeling perched on the bust of a hissing gator, & caught in the coils of the cottonmouth,

basking with the Anhinga & clutched in the hope of the Heron. I wait. I watch. I
wonder, does he see it? The lessons in the endless fields. Until I am no longer sitting

in the passenger seat of the car with mud-tracked Chuck Taylors, where I've lived in patience,
for him to ask me if we could pull off the road if we could watch in silence, hand in hand,

as the grace of the 'Glades unfurls around us, next to one another, holding one another.
People have done this before. We have done this before, but not with one another.

Ode to Laika

Laika, I hope the orbital sunrise
over your never-to-fetch, squeaky
ball Earth gave you the ball chase
of your milk bone-filled dreams.
I hope the cosmic vastness of empty
space let you dream of the largest
black backyard, where you could be
a bullet in your tin sarcophagus for
your space-race squirrel-starred hunt.
Laika, I hope you hit light speed, racing
through the cosmos in the hot pursuit
of treats but instead found your own tail,
ending the circular quest of catching it.
I hope you got the universe's best
belly rub from Jupiter's rings and
that when you barked into the void
you heard whistling and an endless
call of *good girl* and kissy noises.
Laika, I hope the last smooch you
received smelled like a New York
strip smothered in extra smooth
peanut butter topped with bacon.
I hope the surging colors and sparkles
of a supernovas' cosmic-dust wonder
felt better than seeing a lone T-bone
on the Soviet streets of Moscow.
Laika, for what it's worth, I hope
you watch us silly humans explode
and howl at our cheese moon from
the galaxy's comfiest couch knowing,
old girl, that you have become our
timeless cosmonaut, patron saint
of one-way trips and other journeys
from which you can never return.

My Mother Teaches Me to Pick Spanish Moss

She tells me of the red chiggers that we take home
      in fallen moss, berry bugs that die in the cold.

She goes high into the limbs of live oak or
      big cypress trees my small legs and short arms

could not yet reach, climbing for heaven from where I
      watched, dropping wispy moss to me as I folded it

tenderly, tucked snug in her oversized burlap bag
      that hung past my waist to my knees. A plush pillow,

filled with silvery-grey green strands, the fairy hair
      of the trees, at home she places the large copper

pot engraved with Celtic knots mingling with
      intricate flowers on the gas stove and

begins with her fingers, separating
      the folded moss into three piles—one she

will throw in the pot, another tossed in our shoes
      or mattresses, the last, she stores in a jar

for the coming months. She stirs the boiling moss,
      ushering the magic steam up to her face. Moss

she will braid over and over into a wreath until
      her father's death when she will place it in his

shoes, within the seams of his coat pockets,
      to make his final pillow. She prays over the

mason jar of its juice, splashes its tinctured
      water in her scotch when she thinks no one is

looking until she is drunk. She will take me each
      winter until I am grown, and teach me over

and over how to pick Spanish Moss, and tell me
      how she wishes she could still feel the magic

in the land, or the spirits of the swamp.

Inside the Killing Jar

"A killing jar is a device used by entomologists to kill captured insects quickly and with minimum damage."

I stared with wonder at the glass
rested so plainly upon my father's desk.
Smooth-bodied across the top, with a
rounded, almost pursed lip that kissed
the metal lid into place, secure and
suction sealed. The bottom coddled
with cotton, and below a small layer
of plaster molded into it, even and flat;
further below glass incisions, crinkle cut
 marks, patterns made to hold—to grip.

My grubby, chunky baby fingers would
tentacle wrap the jar, cap off, hold it
close and hold it steady, just tight enough.
Alone, I would run and run and run,
circle after circle, line after line,
chasing the colored blur of the butterfly.
The blades of grass, fingers tickling, their
dewdrops lubricated my small hands
until I was just there—
just close enough to—
just within reach of—

the burning orange gold ember that fluttered,
resting upon the blazing star of purple,
planted upright reaching for the last gleam
before eventide. Slowly, trustingly, it flitted
into the smooth glass, my slippery fingers
scrambled for the lid that kissed it into place,
secure and suction sealed. I returned the jar
to my father's desk, where it would sit plainly,
with my discovery nestled and rested upon the
cotton. I stared at it with wonder, and I waited.

He said her name was American Painted Lady,
the lady that evaded me all afternoon, she loved
Liatris. This I was unsure of; I still knew little of
the world. *The Liatris, the blazing star, is a perennial,*
tough, and beautiful. Much like you, he added. This too,
I was unsure of.

Once the darkness crept in, when the moon hid
behind the gray sky when all outside was beginning
to quiet. I checked on her. She looked lifeless,
wings open, but unmoving. I shook the jar, lightly.
I did not want to disturb her. She seemed *dead*, no—
she *was* dead. I screamed for my father.

You wouldn't last very long in the killing jar either, he chided.

Mother took me outside, where she placed my hands,
one over the other almost as if I was ready to receive
communion. She unscrewed the jar, and our lady slowly
swayed down, wilted in my hands. I remember it felt
so light in my palm, just as I had imagined a soul to be.
The white powder from her wings flickered on my
fingertips, her gold embers fading, the eyes on the back
of her wings gazed upon me, unblinking, until I wept.

That night, my mother served cabbage rolls
for dinner, she smoked her cigarette, and my
father read the paper, held his glass, his whiskey
close, and steady. While I sat there silent, staring
at my small hands in wonder, *Would I go to Hell?*
Back then, I still believed nothing went unpunished.

The Crystal Ball
For my Mother

It sits on my desk like it's got secrets
or tax records, or a recipe for being wanted.
I mean, it's technically beautiful—
smooth, glossy, spherical,
like a breast implant for a god
or a weapon designed by a minimalist.
She gave it to me wrapped in tissue paper
that smelled like her purse: Mint gum,
metal, patchouli, cigarettes, gobstoppers,
the uncanny whiff of unresolved feelings

She said, "*It's for clarity.*"
I said "*Thank you*"
which is what you say
when your mother hands you
an orb instead of an apology.
She might as well have handed me
a neon sign that said *FIGURE IT OUT
ON YOUR OWN, HONEY!* and
honestly, I'd still hang it in my bedroom.

For weeks I stared into it
like I was pondering the
metaphysics of abandonment
I tried to see her in there—
not the actual her,
not the woman who skipped
three birthdays and my ballet recital,
but the platinum version: Blonde
hair fanned out like a shampoo
commercial, laughing like I'm
funny, reaching for me with
hands that don't flinch.

But the ball is just a ball,
it doesn't do anything
except reflect the overhead lighting
and occasionally roll onto the floor
like it's trying to escape this whole
situation too.

The ball didn't ask to be involved.
It just got handed to me in a
crinkly bag between a coupon for
Panera and a too-long hug
that felt like a warning.

I stared into it like a 14-year-old
trying to figure out if mascara
could solve maternal absence.
It stared back—
quiet as the space between
"I love you" and "I did what I could"
I wanted it to show me her.
The version who stayed.
The one who remembered my
birthday without Facebook.

Sometimes I imagine the ball warming
in my hands, starting to hum softly
then glowing with a soft uterus-colored
light, then I remember it's likely made of
resin, and probably sourced from Etsy,
over-priced, sold at our local witch shop.

One time I brought a boy home and
he asked if it was a sex thing. I said yes
because that was easier than saying
"Actually, it's a shrine to the woman
who taught me to pretend I'm fine."

I don't want her back, just
a better ending.
One where she bursts out of the ball
like a genie with perfect eyeliner,
says "*Just kidding! Of course, I loved you.
I just didn't know how to show it, so I
left instead.*" Cue applause. Cue the
soft-focus montage. Cue the part where
we braid each other's hair and finally
talk about 2007, or anything at all.

But none of that happens.
Instead, I dust the ball once a week
like a Victorian widow polishing a
tombstone and pretend it's not weird
to keep a decorative orb as a proxy for
a parent's conditional affection.

I keep it anyway.
Not because it's magic
but because it reminds me of her—
all that promise
all that opacity
all that impossible smoothness.

She gave me this, instead of
talking about the time she left
for two years and came back with
new furniture and a boyfriend named
Gary who smelled like motor oil and
gave me a twenty when I cried.

The orb is better than Gary.
It doesn't ask questions. Doesn't make
weird jokes about hormones. Doesn't
suggest I try decaf when I get emotional.

Sometimes I wonder if she gave it to me
because she thought it would make her
seem mysterious. Like, *I'm not distant,
I'm just spiritual.* Like, *I didn't abandon you,
I transcended you.* Honestly? Respect.

The orb keeps secrets.
It knows all about the way I practice
acceptance like a shitty religion.
How I still imagine her knocking on
my door with cake or cookies or closure
wearing that lemon-colored cardigan
she wore the day I almost said, *You left
before I could say the worst parts out loud.*

If I ever become a mother,
I'll give my kid a rock or a
Walkie-talkie or something that
doesn't pretend to be mystical.

I polish it like a relic.
I tell my therapist about it
like it's a recurring dream.
She asks me what I see in it.
I say, *myself.*
She nods like this is progress.
But I say *but smaller, and weirder,*
lit from below, like in horror movies.

Sometimes I carry it around the
apartment like a pet or a grievance.
Sometimes I sit it in the sun and pretend
it's charging. Sometimes I cry in front
of it on purpose, in case it's watching.

And yeah—
sometimes I think about smashing it.
To see if anything comes out.
A letter. A locket. A scrabble piece.
A mother who says *I tried,*
A poem that ends.

But then I don't—
Because even though it's stupid and
heavy and a little bit cursed, it's still
the closest thing I have to her saying:
Here. I thought of you.

In Gratitutde

This chapbook would not have been possible without several remarkable individuals' unwavering support and inspiration.

First and foremost, I would like to express my deepest gratitude to my undergraduate instructors, Julie Marie Wade, Denise Duhamel, Richard Blanco, and Campbell McGrath. Thank you for sharing your passion for poetry, commitment to teaching, and reinvigorating my love for writing poetry. You have continuously shown me the boundless possibilities that dedication and passion can unlock in poetry land. Thank you for holding my hand.

To my graduate thesis committee, Barbara Hamby, Virgil Suarez, and David Kirby—words cannot fully express my appreciation for your unwavering guidance and support. Your profound insights, boundless patience, and steadfast belief in my work have refined my craft and bolstered my confidence as a writer. Each of you has been a beacon of inspiration, pushing me to delve deeper into my creativity and strive for excellence. Barbara, your keen editorial eye and poetic wisdom have refined my craft in ways I never thought possible. Your ability to illuminate the subtleties of language and form has also been transformative, allowing me to discover new dimensions in my poetry. Virgil, your unique perspective and fervent push for authenticity have emboldened me to write with greater honesty and clarity. David, your limitless enthusiasm and insightful critiques have continually inspired me to elevate my work. Your ability to infuse humor and lightheartedness into the craft of poetry has taught me to embrace creativity with both rigor and a sense of fun. I thank each of you for your encouragement and constructive feedback, which have been essential in my development, and I am profoundly grateful for the time and effort you have invested in my growth.

Thank you all for your profound influence on my journey as a poet. Your contributions have been immeasurable, and this chapbook is a testament to your dedication and mentorship. I am beyond grateful for your help in finding my path and encouraging me to explore it confidently, curiously, and passionately.

To my father, thank you for always being there for me. Your constant presence and encouragement have provided the strength and reassurance I needed to pursue my dreams. Thank you for always being my rock. *Sin Duda*

To my family, whose love has been the fertile soil from which my creativity blossoms, thank you for your unwavering support and understanding. Your presence in my life fills each poem with warmth and meaning. I am fortunate beyond words to have you by my side, cheering me on with every line penned.

To all of you, this collection is just as much yours as it is mine.

Chloe Rodríguez is a poet, writer, translator, and instructor from South Florida, where the salt air clings to everything and memory behaves like weather. She holds an MFA in Creative Writing from Florida State University and is currently pursuing her PhD in Creative Writing. Her poems linger in the soft violences of nostalgia, the shimmering ghosts of girlhood, and the strange, devotional rituals of longing.

A Pushcart Prize nominee, her work has appeared in *Delta Review, Wingless Dreamer, The Windward Review, Poet's Choice, Midnight Mind Magazine, The South Florida Poetry Journal's Anthology of Florida Poets,* and elsewhere. Her debut chapbook, *Ruin Me Before the Party Ends*, arrives courtesy of Finishing Line Press.

She is at work on both a full-length poetry collection and a memoir-in-progress, writing toward a life split between languages, landscapes, and the eternal dream of a swampside hermitage somewhere deep in the Everglades—where she hopes, one day, to retreat and spend her days writing, translating, and swatting mosquitos like the feral poet she was always meant to be.